THE ELT GRAPHIC NOVEL
William Shakespeare

ELT VERSION

Script by John McDonald

Adapted for ELT by Brigit Viney

NATIONAL GEOGRAPHIC
LEARNING

Australia · Brazil · Mexico · Singapore · United Kingdom · United States

Macbeth:
The ELT Graphic Novel
William Shakespeare

Script by John McDonald
Adapted for ELT by
Brigit Viney

Publisher: Bryan Fletcher

Editor in Chief: Clive Bryant

Development Editor:
  Jennifer Nunan

Content Project Editor:
  Natalie Griffith

Pencils: Neill Cameron

Inks: Bambos

Colouring: Jason Cardy and
  Kat Nicholson

Lettering: Nigel Dobbyn

Contributing Writer:
  Amanda Cole

Manufacturing Manager:
  Helen Mason

Marketing Manager:
  Marcin Wojtynski

Cover / Text Designer:
  Jo Wheeler

Compositor: Jo Wheeler and

Parkwood Composition
  Service, Inc.

Audio: EFS Television
  Production Ltd.

Published in association with
Classical Comics Ltd.

Images on pages 3 & 6
reproduced with the kind
permission of the Trustees of
the National Library of
Scotland. © National Library
of Scotland.

For product information and technology assistance,
contact us at
**Cengage Learning Customer & Sales Support,
cengage.com/contact**
For permission to use material from this text or product,
submit all requests online at **cengage.com/permissions**
Further permissions questions can be emailed to
permissionrequest@cengage.com

ISBN-13: 978-1-4240-2870-2 [with audio]
ISBN-10: 1-4240-2870-1

ISBN-13: 978-1-4240-2872-6 [without audio]
ISBN-10: 1-4240-2872-8

National Geographic Learning
Cheriton House, North Way, Andover, Hampshire, SP10 5BE
United Kingdom

National Geographic Learning, a Cengage Learning Company, has a mission to bring the world to the classroom and the classroom to life. With our English language programs, students learn about their world by experiencing it. Through our partnerships with National Geographic and TED Talks, they develop the language and skills they need to be successful global citizens and leaders.

Locate your local office at **international.cengage.com/region**

Visit National Geographic Learning online at
NGL.Cengage.com/ELT
Visit our corporate website at **www.cengage.com**

Printed in China by RR Donnelley
Print Number: 10   Print Year: 2018

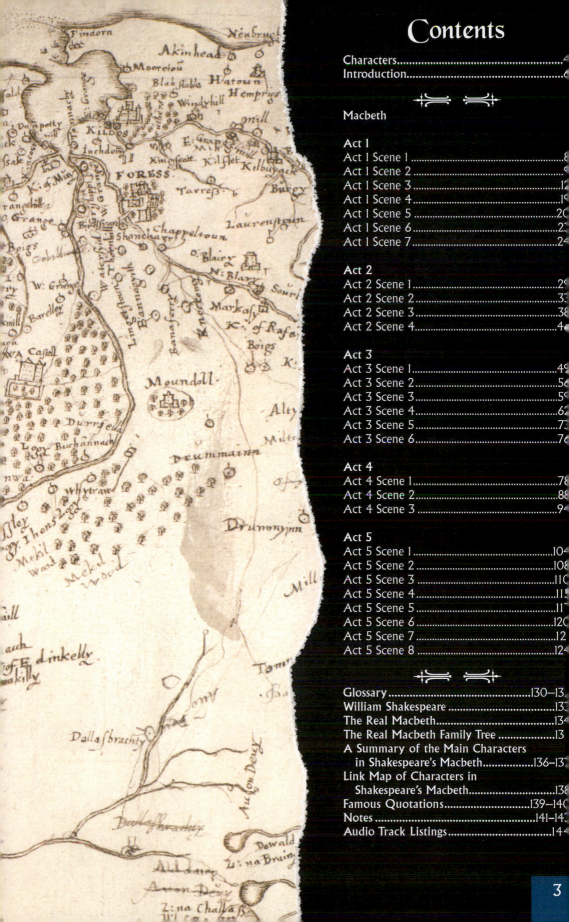
Contents

Characters

Duncan
King of Scotland

Malcolm
Son of Duncan

Donalbain
Son of Duncan

Macduff
Nobleman *of Scotland*

Lenox
Nobleman of Scotland

Rosse
Nobleman of Scotland

Lady Macbeth
Wife of Macbeth

Lady Macduff
Wife of Macduff

Siward
Leader of the English **Army**

A lady who **serves**
Lady Macbeth

Seyton
A man who serves Macbeth

An English Doctor

A Scottish Doctor

A **Porter**

An Old Man

First Murderer

Second Murderer

Third Murderer

Characters

Macbeth
A leader in the King's Army

Banquo
A leader in the King's Army

The Ghost of Banquo

Menteth
Nobleman of Scotland

Angus
Nobleman of Scotland

Cathness
Nobleman of Scotland

Young Siward
Son of Siward

Fleance
Son of Banquo

Boy
Son of Macduff

First Witch

Second Witch

Third Witch

Hecate
The 'Queen' Witch

and **Lords,** Ladies,
Officers, Soldiers,
Messengers, Ghosts
and **Spirits**.

Introduction

t is Scotland in the year 1040.

King Duncan has **ruled** the land for six years, since the death of his grandfather. He is a good king but Scotland is not a peaceful country. It has been divided in two for centuries. **Vikings** live in the north, and **Saxons** live in the south. Each small group of Vikings or Saxons has its own strong leader who is a great fighter.

Now that Duncan is king, all the different groups have a chance to come together and form a single nation. However, some leaders do not welcome this. They want to remain independent and they continue to fight against Duncan. Sometimes they are joined by groups of fighters from Ireland and Norway. Some of them would even like to be King of Scotland themselves.

Duncan sends a powerful **army** to fight against these groups who do not accept him as king. The army is led by a number of **noblemen** who are experienced soldiers. The greatest and most trusted of these is King Duncan's cousin. This is the **Thane** of Glamis, whose name is …

.. Macbeth.

An empty, open place ...

CRAAACKKKK!!!!

WHEN SHALL WE THREE MEET AGAIN? IN HEAVY STORM OR POURING RAIN?

WHEN ONE SIDE'S LOST AND THE OTHER'S WON.

BEFORE THE SETTING OF THE SUN.

WHERE?

ON THE HEATH.

TO MEET WITH MACBETH.

FAIR IS DARK, AND DARK IS FAIR. FLYING THROUGH THE DIRTY AIR.

AND *THANE* OF CAWDOR.

THAT'S WHAT THEY SAID!

WHO'S THIS?

THE KING IS *DELIGHTED* WITH THE NEWS OF YOUR SUCCESS, MACBETH.

HE HAS SENT US TO TAKE YOU TO HIM.

HE'S DECIDED TO MAKE YOU THANE OF CAWDOR.

WHAT! CAN THE *DEVIL* SPEAK THE TRUTH?

BUT THE THANE OF CAWDOR IS STILL ALIVE.

HE WILL DIE SOON BECAUSE HE FOUGHT AGAINST THE KING.

GLAMIS AND CAWDOR. THE GREATEST WILL FOLLOW.

THANK YOU.

The King's *palace* at Forres. King Duncan is waiting for Macbeth and Banquo ...

IS CAWDOR DEAD?

YES, MY *LORD.* THEY SAY THAT HE ASKED FOR *YOUR HIGHNESS'S FORGIVENESS* AND THAT HE WAS DEEPLY SORRY.

HE DIED VERY *BRAVELY.*

I TRUSTED HIM SO MUCH.

MY DEAR COUSIN!

I CAN NEVER REPAY YOU FOR WHAT YOU'VE DONE!

I WAS JUST DOING MY DUTY, YOUR HIGHNESS.

I'LL MAKE SURE YOU BECOME A GREAT MAN.

AND YOU TOO, BANQUO.

I ONLY WANT TO *SERVE* YOU, MY LORD.

I HAVE SOMETHING TO TELL EVERYONE.

I'VE CHOSEN MY *ELDEST* SON, MALCOLM, TO BE KING AFTER ME. FROM NOW ON, HIS *TITLE* WILL BE THE PRINCE OF CUMBERLAND.

NOW, LET'S GO TO INVERNESS AND VISIT YOUR CASTLE.

I'LL GO ON AHEAD, TO TELL MY WIFE.

MALCOLM! HE'S IN MY WAY NOW. I DON'T WANT TO THINK ABOUT WHAT I MIGHT DO ...

LET'S QUICKLY FOLLOW MACBETH TO HIS CASTLE.

Act One — Scene Five

At Macbeth's castle, in Inverness, Lady Macbeth receives news from her husband ...

'THREE *WITCHES* TOLD ME I WOULD BE *THANE* OF CAWDOR. THEN I WAS MADE THANE OF CAWDOR.'

'THEY ALSO TOLD ME I WOULD BE KING! I HAD TO TELL YOU IMMEDIATELY, MY DEAREST.'

YOU'RE THANE OF GLAMIS AND CAWDOR! AND YOU WILL BE KING! BUT YOU'RE TOO KIND TO DO WHAT YOU HAVE TO DO TO BECOME KING.

WHAT YOU WANT ISN'T YOURS. TO GET IT, YOU'LL HAVE TO DO SOMETHING THAT YOU'RE AFRAID TO DO.

HURRY HOME. I'LL MAKE SURE NOTHING GETS IN THE WAY OF OUR GOLDEN FUTURE.

THANE OF GLAMIS! AND THANE OF CAWDOR! YOUR LETTER HAS MADE ME SO HAPPY.

DUNCAN'S COMING HERE TONIGHT, MY LOVE.

AND WHEN IS HE LEAVING?

TOMORROW.

HE'LL NEVER SEE TOMORROW! YOU MUSTN'T LET PEOPLE KNOW WHAT YOU'RE PLANNING. YOU MUST WELCOME HIM PROPERLY ...

... AND GIVE HIM DINNER. LEAVE THE REAL BUSINESS OF THE NIGHT TO ME.

WE'LL TALK LATER.

JUST BE CLEAR IN YOUR MIND. LEAVE THE REST TO ME.

OUR LOVELY *HOSTESS!* THANK YOU FOR DOING SO MUCH FOR US.

WE CAN NEVER DO ENOUGH TO THANK YOU FOR WHAT YOU HAVE GIVEN US.

WHERE'S THE *THANE* OF CAWDOR? HE RODE MUCH FASTER THAN US.

HE WELCOMES YOU HERE, *YOUR HIGHNESS.* WE ARE YOUR *SERVANTS* FOREVER.

PLEASE TAKE ME TO HIM.

Act One
Scene Seven

A great dinner for the King ...

STOP! I'M NOT AFRAID TO ACT AS A MAN.

WHEN YOU PROMISED ME YOU WOULD DO IT, THEN YOU WERE A MAN. NOW YOU ARE JUST MAKING EXCUSES.

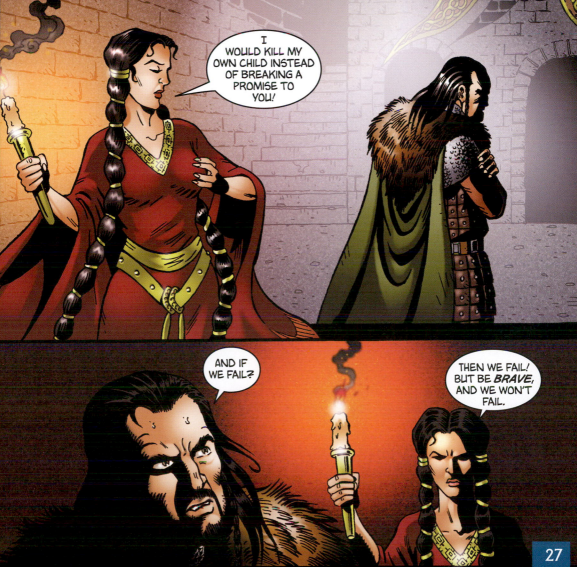

I WOULD KILL MY OWN CHILD INSTEAD OF BREAKING A PROMISE TO YOU!

AND IF WE FAIL?

THEN WE FAIL! BUT BE *BRAVE*, AND WE WON'T FAIL.

I DREAMT ABOUT THE THREE **WITCHES** LAST NIGHT.

I DON'T THINK ABOUT THEM. BUT WHEN WE HAVE TIME, WE CAN TALK ABOUT THEM – IF YOU WANT TO.

WHEN IT SUITS YOU.

IF YOU CAN WAIT UNTIL I'M READY, THAT WOULD BE GOOD OF YOU.

I'LL LISTEN TO YOU, IF WHAT YOU SAY ISN'T SOMETHING I'M UNEASY ABOUT.

SLEEP WELL.

THANKS. YOU TOO.

Later ...

THE *WINE* THAT MADE THEM DRUNK HAS MADE ME *BRAVE*. MACBETH'S MURDERING THE KING RIGHT NOW.

WHO'S THERE? WHO IS IT?

OH NO! THEY'VE WOKEN UP! I LEFT THEIR *DAGGERS* READY FOR HIM. THEY WERE EASY FOR HIM TO SEE.

MY HUSBAND!

I'VE DONE IT.

33

HELP ME!

HELP THE LADY!

WE MUST TAKE CONTROL OF THIS SITUATION.

DON'T SAY ANYTHING, WE MAY PUT OURSELVES IN DANGER. LET'S LEAVE. IT'S TOO SOON FOR US TO BE CRYING FOR OUR FATHER.

YES. WE HAVEN'T STARTED TO REALLY FEEL SAD YET.

LOOK AFTER THE LADY!

LET'S GET DRESSED AND THEN MEET. WE MUST FIND OUT WHAT HAPPENED. I WANT TO FIGHT WHOEVER DID THIS.

SO DO I.

WE ALL DO!

LET'S MEET IN THE GREAT HALL.

YES!

NOT US. I'LL GO TO ENGLAND. WHAT WILL YOU DO?

I'LL GO TO IRELAND. WE'LL BE SAFER IF WE AREN'T TOGETHER. HERE THERE ARE KNIVES IN MEN'S SMILES.

YES, IT'S TOO DANGEROUS HERE.

LET'S GET OUR HORSES AND GO!

DO THEY KNOW WHO MURDERED THE KING?

THE MEN MACBETH KILLED.

WHY DID THEY DO IT?

THEY WERE PAID TO DO IT. THE KING'S SONS HAVE RUN AWAY. MAYBE THEY PAID THE MURDERERS.

THAT'S TERRIBLE! TO KILL YOUR OWN FATHER! MACBETH WILL PROBABLY BECOME KING THEN.

HE'S ALREADY GONE TO SCONE FOR THE CEREMONY.

ARE YOU GOING TO SCONE?

NO, I'M GOING HOME TO FIFE.

Act Three
Scene One

Macbeth is now King of Scotland. In the King's *palace* at Forres, Banquo thinks Macbeth has done something wrong ...

TRUMPET!

TRUMPET!

HERE'S OUR MOST IMPORTANT GUEST.

OUR CELEBRATION WOULDN'T BE COMPLETE WITHOUT HIM.

YOU HAVE IT ALL NOW, AS THE *WITCHES* PROMISED. I THINK YOU HAVE DONE SOMETHING TERRIBLE TO GET IT.

BUT IF THEY WERE RIGHT ABOUT YOU, THEN THEY MIGHT BE RIGHT ABOUT ME.

WE'RE HAVING A GREAT DINNER TONIGHT, AND WE'D LIKE YOU TO BE THERE.

OF COURSE.

49

ARE YOU GOING RIDING THIS AFTERNOON?

YES, I AM.

ARE YOU GOING TO RIDE FAR?

AS FAR AS I CAN BEFORE DINNER.

DON'T MISS OUR DINNER.

NO, I WON'T.

I HEAR DUNCAN'S SONS ARE HIDING IN ENGLAND AND IRELAND. THEY'RE SAYING THAT THEY DIDN'T KILL THEIR FATHER AND THEY'RE TELLING TERRIBLE LIES. BUT I'LL TELL YOU ABOUT THAT TOMORROW.

IS FLEANCE GOING WITH YOU?

YES. WE MUST GO.

GO SAFELY.

GOODBYE.

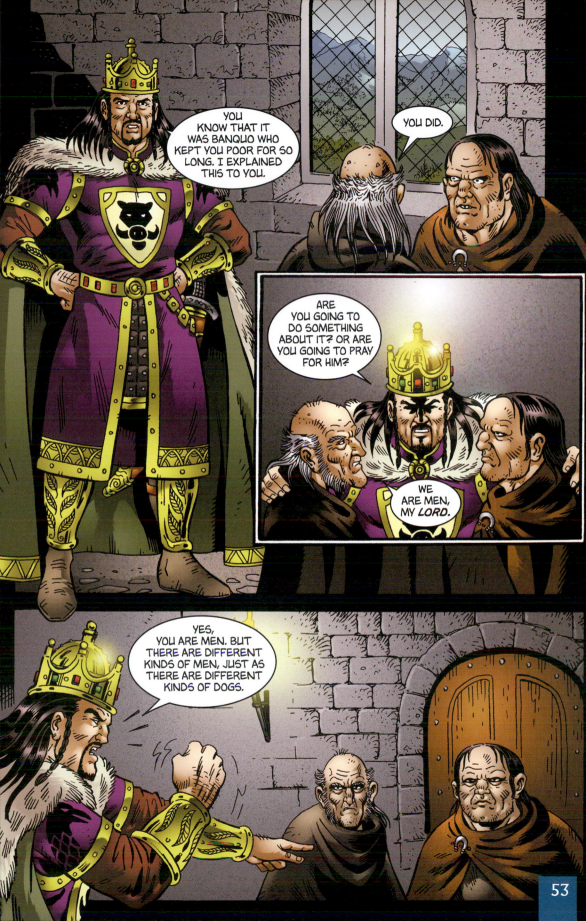

WHO PUT THE LIGHT OUT?

WASN'T THAT THE PLAN?

ONLY ONE OF THEM IS DEAD. THE SON HAS ESCAPED.

WE'VE ONLY DONE HALF THE JOB.

WELL, LET'S GO AND TELL MACBETH WHAT WE HAVE DONE.

WHY ARE YOU SO FRIGHTENED? IT'S JUST A CHAIR.
LOOK! SEE!
SPEAK!
HAVE YOU GONE MAD?
I SAW HIM. HE WAS THERE.
SHAME ON YOU!
THERE HAVE BEEN MURDERS BEFORE, AND THE DEAD STAYED DEAD ...

GOODNIGHT! GOODNIGHT!

I WILL BE PUNISHED. BLOOD WILL HAVE BLOOD, THEY SAY.

WHAT'S THE TIME?

IT'S ALMOST MORNING.

MACDUFF REFUSED TO COME TO THE DINNER.

WHY?

I DON'T KNOW, BUT I'LL FIND OUT. SOMEONE IN HIS HOUSE WILL TELL ME.

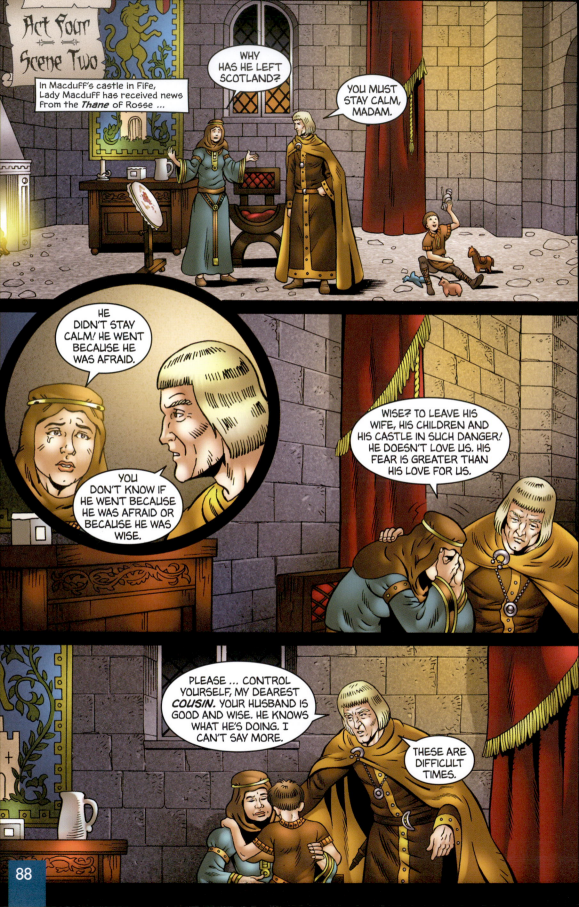

89

93

In the garden of King Edward's *palace* in England. Malcolm, the son of Duncan, is talking to Macduff, the *Thane* of Fife ...

LET'S TALK SOMEWHERE QUIET.

LET'S GO AND DEFEND OUR COUNTRY. TERRIBLE THINGS ARE HAPPENING THERE.

I'LL FIGHT FOR WHAT I KNOW IS TRUE. WHAT YOU HAVE SAID MAY BE TRUE. BUT IN THE PAST WE THOUGHT MACBETH WAS HONEST.

YOU YOURSELF LOVED HIM AND HE HASN'T HURT YOU YET. MAYBE YOU'RE TRYING TO PLEASE HIM BY LYING TO ME.

I'M NOT A LIAR!

BUT MACBETH IS. AND A GOOD, HONEST NATURE LIKE YOURS MAY GIVE IN TO PRESSURE FROM A KING.

THAT'S THE END OF MY HOPES, THEN.

I DON'T UNDERSTAND WHY YOU LEFT YOUR WIFE AND CHILDREN SO QUICKLY. I'M SORRY, BUT I HAVE TO BE CAREFUL.

95

MACDUFF! YOU'VE SHOWN ME YOU'RE HONEST. MACBETH'S TRIED TO TRICK ME BEFORE, SO I HAD TO TEST YOU.

FORGET WHAT I SAID ABOUT MYSELF. I'M NOT LIKE THAT AT ALL.

BEFORE YOU CAME, I WAS READY TO GO TO SCOTLAND WITH TEN THOUSAND MEN.

NOW WE CAN GO TOGETHER!

WHY DON'T YOU SAY SOMETHING?

IT'S HARD TO KNOW WHAT TO BELIEVE.

WAIT A MOMENT.

An English doctor approaches ...

IS THE KING GOING TO COME OUT?

YES. THERE ARE A LOT OF SICK PEOPLE WHO ARE WAITING FOR HIM. THEIR ILLNESS DEFEATS OUR MEDICINE, BUT HE CAN MAKE THEM BETTER.

THANK YOU, DOCTOR.

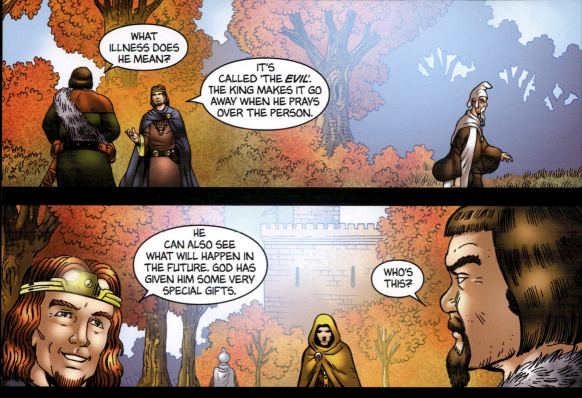

WHAT ILLNESS DOES HE MEAN?

IT'S CALLED 'THE *EVIL*'. THE KING MAKES IT GO AWAY WHEN HE PRAYS OVER THE PERSON.

HE CAN ALSO SEE WHAT WILL HAPPEN IN THE FUTURE. GOD HAS GIVEN HIM SOME VERY SPECIAL GIFTS.

WHO'S THIS?

I DON'T KNOW.

IT'S MY *COUSIN*!

AH, WELCOME, ROSSE!

THANK YOU, SIR.

ARE THINGS STILL THE SAME IN SCOTLAND?

THEY'RE TERRIBLE. THERE IS SO MUCH KILLING THAT NOBODY NOTICES IT ANY MORE.

IT'S TRUE.

WHAT IS THE LATEST *HORROR?*

THERE'S A NEW ONE EVERY MINUTE.

HOW ARE MY WIFE AND CHILDREN?

THEY'RE ... WELL.

MACBETH HASN'T ATTACKED THEM?

NO. THEY WERE FINE ... WHEN I LEFT THEM.

TELL ME MORE. HOW ARE THINGS?

Act Five
Scene One

Late at night in Dunsinane Castle ...

I'VE BEEN HERE FOR TWO NIGHTS BUT I'VE SEEN NOTHING. WHEN DID SHE LAST WALK?

SINCE THE KING WENT TO WAR, SHE'S DONE IT. SHE GETS OUT OF BED, UNLOCKS HER CUPBOARD, TAKES OUT SOME PAPER, WRITES ON IT, READS IT AND THEN GOES BACK TO BED. ALL THE TIME SHE'S ASLEEP.

DOES SHE SAY ANYTHING?

I WON'T REPEAT WHAT SHE SAYS, SIR.

YOU CAN TELL ME. AND YOU SHOULD.

NO, SIR. I WON'T TELL ANYONE.

LOOK, HERE SHE COMES.

She's asleep. Watch her.

Did you hear that?

THE *THANE* OF FIFE HAD A WIFE. WHERE IS SHE NOW?

WILL THESE HANDS NEVER BE CLEAN?

NO MORE OF THAT, MY *LORD.* DON'T BE SO NERVOUS.

Oh dear! You have seen things you shouldn't see.

She's certainly said things she shouldn't say. *Heaven* knows what she has seen.

I CAN STILL SMELL THE BLOOD. NOTHING WILL MAKE MY LITTLE HAND SMELL SWEET AGAIN. OOOHHH!!!

She's very troubled.

I wouldn't like to be her.

Will she be all right?

I don't know. But I've known some people who have walked in their sleep and who have been all right.

WASH YOUR HANDS! DON'T LOOK SO FRIGHTENED.

BANQUO'S DEAD.

Not that too?

LET'S GO TO BED. SOMEONE'S KNOCKING AT THE GATE.

COME, GIVE ME YOUR HAND.

WILL SHE GO BACK TO BED NOW?

YES.

ALL THESE TERRIBLE EVENTS CAN CAUSE MADNESS LIKE THIS. THEN PEOPLE WITH SICK MINDS TELL THEIR SECRETS TO THEIR PILLOWS.

LOOK AFTER HER. MAKE SURE SHE CAN'T HURT HERSELF AND WATCH HER ALL THE TIME. GOODNIGHT. I WON'T SAY WHAT I'M THINKING.

GOODNIGHT, DOCTOR.

DON'T LOOK SO WHITE AND AFRAID! WHAT SOLDIERS, MILK-FACE?

ENGLISH SOLDIERS.

GET OUT OF HERE!

SEYTON!

IT MAKES ME SICK WHEN –

SEYTON!

MY TIME HAS COME. BUT I'VE LIVED LONG ENOUGH, AND I KNOW I WON'T HAVE ANYTHING GOOD IN MY OLD AGE. PEOPLE WILL HATE ME.

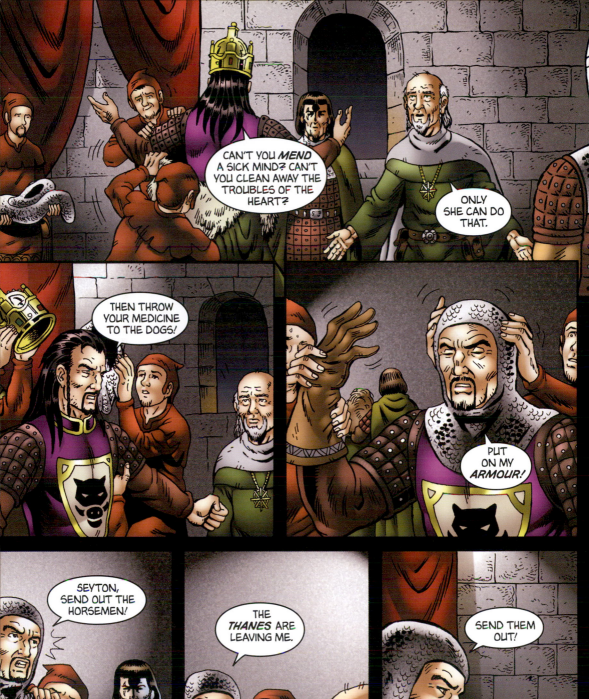

CAN'T YOU *MEND* A SICK MIND? CAN'T YOU CLEAN AWAY THE TROUBLES OF THE HEART?

ONLY SHE CAN DO THAT.

THEN THROW YOUR MEDICINE TO THE DOGS!

PUT ON MY *ARMOUR!*

SEYTON, SEND OUT THE HORSEMEN!

THE *THANES* ARE LEAVING ME.

SEND THEM OUT!

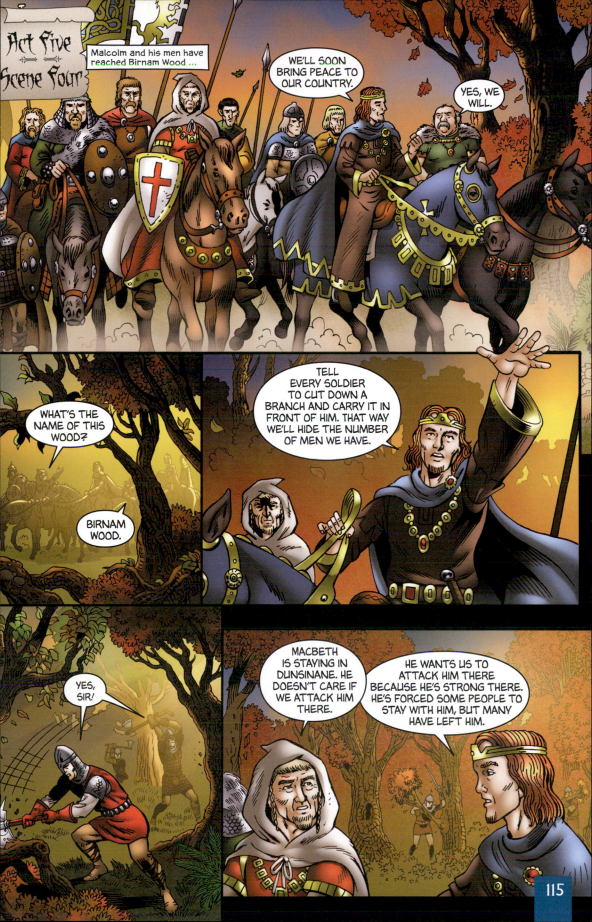

SCREAMS LIKE THAT USED TO MAKE ME FRIGHTENED. BUT I'VE SEEN SO MUCH *HORROR* RECENTLY THAT NOTHING BOTHERS ME NOW.

Moments later...

WHAT WAS THAT CRY FOR?

THE QUEEN... IS DEAD, MY *LORD*.

HER LIFE HAS ENDED TOO SOON. BUT WHAT DOES IT MATTER?

TOMORROW, AND TOMORROW, AND TOMORROW. EACH DAY SHOWS US THE WAY TO DEATH.

AND NOW HER SMALL CANDLE IS OUT.

LIFE IS JUST A WALKING SHADOW. IT'S A STORY THAT A FOOL TELLS — FULL OF NOISE BUT WITH NO MEANING.

TELL ME WHAT'S HAPPENING!

I DON'T KNOW HOW TO DESCRIBE WHAT I SAW.

JUST SAY IT!

I LOOKED TOWARDS BIRNAM AND SUDDENLY THE WOOD BEGAN TO MOVE.

LIAR!

IT'S LESS THAN THREE MILES AWAY. IT'S A MOVING WOOD.

IF YOU'RE LYING, I'LL HANG YOU FROM THE NEAREST TREE ...

THE SPIRIT SAID, 'DON'T WORRY UNTIL BIRNAM WOOD COMES TO DUNSINANE'. AND NOW THAT'S HAPPENING!

PREPARE FOR BATTLE! IF WHAT HE SAYS IS TRUE, I CAN'T RUN AWAY.

AT LEAST I'LL DIE WITH ARMOUR ON MY BACK!

Glossary

A

admit /æd'mɪt/ — (admits, admitting, admitted)
If you admit that something bad or embarrassing is true, you agree, often reluctantly, that it is true.

armour / 'aːmə/ In former times, armour was the protective metal clothing worn by soldiers.

army / 'aːmi/ — (armies) An army is a large organised group of people who are armed and trained to fight.

B

bang /bæŋ/ A bang is a sudden loud noise such as an explosion.

battle /'bætəl/ In a war, a battle is a fight between armies or between groups of ships or planes.

battlefield /'bætəlfiːld/ —(battlefields) A battlefield is a place where a battle is fought.

bell /bel/ — (bells) A bell is a hollow metal object with a loose piece hanging inside that hits the sides and makes a sound.

betray /bɪ'treɪ/ — (betrays, betraying, betrayed)
1. If you betray someone who trusts you, you do something which hurts and disappoints them.
2. If someone betrays their country or their comrades, they give information to an enemy, putting their country's security or their comrades' safety at risk.

brave /breɪv/ Someone who is brave is willing to do dangerous things, and does not show fear in difficult or dangerous situations.

bravely /breɪvli/ Someone who does something bravely is a person who does not show fear in difficult or dangerous situations.

bubble /'bʌbəl/ — (bubbles, bubbling, bubbled) When a liquid bubbles, bubbles (pockets of air) move in it, for example because it is boiling or moving quickly.

C

cave /keɪv/ — (caves) A cave is a large hole in the side of a cliff or hill, or under the ground.

cousin /'kʌzən/ — (cousins) Your cousin is the child of your uncle or aunt.

coward /kaʊəd/ — (cowards) A coward is someone who is easily frightened and avoids dangerous or difficult situations.

crack /kræk/ A crack is a sharp sound, like the sound of a piece of wood breaking.

crash /kræʃ/ — (crashes, crashing, crashed) To crash means to move or fall violently, making a sudden loud noise, called a crash.

curse /kɜːs/ — (curses, cursing, cursed) If you curse someone or something, you say insulting things to them or complain strongly about them because you are angry with them.

D

dagger /'dægə/ — (daggers) A dagger is a weapon like a knife with two sharp edges.

delighted /dɪ'laɪtɪd/ If you are delighted, you are extremely pleased and excited about something.

devil /'devəl/ — (devils) A devil is an evil spirit.

diamond /'daɪəmənd/ — (diamonds) A diamond is a hard bright precious stone.

dong /dɒŋ/ A dong is the deep sound of a large bell.

dragon /'drægən/ — (dragons) In stories and legends, a dragon is an animal like a big lizard. It has wings and claws, and breathes out fire.

drum /drʌm/ — (drums) A drum is a musical instrument consisting of a skin stretched tightly over a round frame.

E

eldest /'eldɪst/ The eldest person in a group is the one who was born before all the others.

enemy /'enəmi/ — (enemies) Your enemy is someone who intends to harm you.

evil /'iːvəl/ — (evils) Evil is used to refer to all the wicked and bad things that happen in the world. An evil is a very unpleasant or harmful situation or activity.

F

flag /flæg/ — (flags) A flag is a piece of coloured cloth used as a sign for something or as a signal.

forgiveness /fə'gɪvnɪs/ Forgiveness is the act of forgiving. If you forgive someone who has done something wrong, you stop being angry with them.

G

gather /'gæðə/ – (gathers, gathering, gathered) When people gather somewhere, or if someone gathers them there, they come together in a group.

gentleman /'dʒentəlmən/ – (gentlemen) You can refer politely to men as gentlemen.

greedy /'griːdi/ – (greedier, greediest) Someone who is greedy wants more of something than is necessary or fair.

H

hail /heɪl/ – (hails, hailing, hailed) If a person or event is hailed as important or successful, they are praised publicly.

health /helθ/ Health is a state in which you are fit and well.

heaven /'hevən/ – (heavens) In some religions, heaven is said to be the place where God lives and where good people go when they die.

hedgehog /'hedʒhɒg/ – (hedgehogs) A hedgehog is a small brown animal with sharp spikes covering its back.

hell /hel/ – (hells) You can use *from hell* after a noun when you are emphasising that something or someone is extremely unpleasant or evil.

horrible /'hɒrɪbəl/ If you say that someone or something is horrible, you mean that they are very unpleasant.

horror /'hɒrə/ – (horrors) Horror is a strong feeling of alarm caused by something extremely unpleasant.

hostess /'həʊstɪs/ – (hostesses) The hostess at a party is the woman who has invited the guests and provides the food, drink or entertainment.

L

lion-hearted /laɪən hɑːtɪd/ Someone who is lion-hearted is brave and generous.

lord /lɔːd/ – (lords)

1. In Britain, a lord is a man who has a high rank in the nobility.

2. Lord is a title used in front of the names of some male members of the nobility, and of judges, bishops and some high ranking officials.

M

master /'mɑːstə, 'mæstə/ – (masters) A servant's master is the man that he or she works for.

mend /mend/ – (mends, mending, mended) If you mend something that is damaged or broken, you repair it so that it works properly or can be used.

messenger /'mesɪndʒə/ (messengers) A messenger takes a message to someone, or takes messages regularly as their job.

N

nobleman /'nəʊbəlmən/ – (noblemen) If someone is a nobleman, he belongs to a high social class and has a title.

nut /nʌt/ – (nuts) The firm shelled fruit of some trees and bushes are called nuts.

P

palace /'pælɪs/ – (palaces) A palace is a very large splendid house, especially the home of a king, queen or president.

porter /'pɔːtə/ – (porters) A porter is a person whose job is to carry things, for example people's luggage at a railway station.

pour /pɔː/ – (pours, pouring, poured)

1. If you pour a liquid, you make it flow steadily out of a container by holding the container at an angle.

2. When it rains heavily, you can describe it is as *pouring rain.*

R

revenge /rɪ'vendʒ/ Revenge involves hurting someone who has hurt you.

rule /ruːl/ – (rules, ruling, ruled) The person or group that rules a country controls its affairs.

S

Saxon /'sæksən/ – (Saxons) A Saxon is a person belonging to the Germanic people that conquered parts of England.

scream /skriːm/ – (screams, screaming, screamed) When someone screams, they make a loud high-pitched cry, called a scream, usually because they are in pain or frightened.

servant /'sɜːvənt/ — (servants) A servant is someone who is employed to work in another person's house, for example to cook or clean.

serve /sɜːv/ — (serves, serving, served) If you serve your country, an organisation, or a person, you do useful work for them.

shriek /ʃriːk/ (shrieks, shrieking, shrieked) If you shriek, you give a sudden loud scream, called a shriek.

slap /slæp/ (slaps, slapping, slapped) If you slap someone, or if you give them a slap, you hit them with the palm of your hand.

smash /smæʃ/ — (smashes, smashing, smashed) If something smashes, or if you smash it, it breaks into many pieces, for example when it is hit or dropped.

spirit /'spɪrɪt/ — (spirits)
1. A person's spirit is a part of them that is not physical and that is believed to remain alive after their death.
2. A spirit is a ghost or supernatural being.

stupid /'stjuːpɪd/ — (stupider, stupidest) If you say that someone or something is stupid, you mean that they show a lack of good judgement or intelligence and they are not at all sensible.

surrender /sə'rendə/ —(surrenders, surrendering, surrendered) If you surrender, you stop fighting or resisting someone or something and agree that you have been beaten. Surrender is the act of surrendering.

sword /sɔːd/ (swords) A sword is a weapon with a handle and a long blade.

thane /θeɪn/ — (thanes) A thane is a man ranking between ordinary freemen and nobles, and is granted land by the king or by lords for military service.

thud /θʌd/ — (thuds, thudding, thudded) A thud is a dull sound, usually made by a solid, heavy object hitting something soft. If something thuds somewhere, it makes this sound as it hits it.

thump /θʌmp/ — (thumps, thumping, thumped) If you thump something somewhere, or if it thumps there, it hits something else with a loud, dull sound called a thump.

title /'taɪtəl/ — (titles) Someone's title is a word such as 'Lord' or 'Mrs' that is used before their name to show their status or profession.

toad /təʊd/ — (toads) A toad is an animal like a frog, but with a drier skin.

toil /tɔɪl/ — (toils, toiling, toiled) If you say that people toil, or if you describe their work as toil, you mean that they work hard doing unpleasant or tiring tasks.

traitor /'treɪtə/ — (traitors) A traitor is someone who betrays their country or a group of which they are a member by helping their enemies.

trumpet /'trʌmpɪt/ — (trumpets) A trumpet is a brass wind instrument.

U

uncle /'ʌŋkəl/ — (uncles) Your uncle is the brother of your mother or father, or the husband of your aunt.

V

iking /'vaɪkɪŋ/ — (Vikings) A Viking is any of the Scandinavian sea pirates who raided and settled in parts of northwestern Europe in the 8th to 11th century.

W

weapon /'wepən/ — (weapons) A weapon is an object such as a gun, knife or missile.

wine /waɪn/ — (wines) Wine is an alcoholic drink, usually made from grapes.

witch /wɪtʃ/ — (witches) A witch is a woman who is believed to have magic powers, especially evil ones.

Y

Your Highness /jɔː 'haɪnɪs/ — (Highnesses) You use expressions such as Your Highness and His Highness to address or refer to a member of a royal family.

William Shakespeare

(c. 1564 - 1616 AD)

Many people believe that William Shakespeare was the greatest writer in the English language. He wrote 38 plays, 154 sonnets and five poems. His plays have been translated into every major living language.

The actual date of Shakespeare's birth is unknown. Most people accept that his birthday was April 23rd, 1564. He died on the same date, 52 years later.

The life of William Shakespeare can be divided into three acts. He lived in the small village of Stratford-upon-Avon until he was 20 years old. There, he studied, got married and had children. Then Shakespeare lived as an actor and playwright (writer of plays) in London. Finally, when he was about 50, Shakespeare retired back to his hometown. He enjoyed some wealth gained from his successful years of work — but died a few years later.

William Shakespeare was the eldest son of tradesman John Shakespeare and Mary Arden. He was the third of eight children. William Shakespeare was lucky to survive childhood. Sixteenth century England was filled with diseases such as smallpox, tuberculosis, typhus and dysentery. The average length of life was 35 years. Three of Shakespeare's seven siblings died from what was probably the Bubonic Plague.

Few records exist about Shakespeare's life. According to most accounts, he went to the local grammar school and studied English literature and Latin. When he was 18 years old, he married Anne Hathaway. She was a local farmer's daughter. They had three children: Susanna in 1583, and twins Hamnet and Judith in 1585. Hamnet, Shakespeare's only son, died when he was 11.

Shakespeare moved to London in 1587. He was an actor at The Globe Theatre. This was one of the largest theatres in England. He appeared in public as a poet in 1593. Later on, in 1599, he became part-owner of The Globe.

When Queen Elizabeth died in 1603, her cousin James became King. He supported Shakespeare and his actors. He allowed them to be called the 'King's Men' as long as they entertained the court.

During 1590 and 1613, Shakespeare wrote his plays, sonnets and poems. The first plays are thought to have been comedies and histories. He was to become famous for both types of writing. Next, he mainly wrote tragedies until about 1608. These included *Hamlet, King Lear* and *Macbeth,* which are considered three of the best examples of writing in the English language. In his last phase, Shakespeare wrote tragicomedies, also known as romances. His final play was *Henry VII,* written two years before his death.

Shakespeare's cause of death is unknown. He was buried at the Church of the Holy Trinity in Stratford-upon-Avon. His gravestone has the words (believed to have been written by Shakespeare himself) on it:

Good friend for Jesus sake forbear,
To dig the dust enclosed here!
Blessed be the man that spares these stones,
And cursed be he that moves my bones.

In his will, Shakespeare left most of his possessions to his eldest daughter, Susanna. He left his wife, Anne, his 'second best bed' — but nobody knows what this gift meant. Shakespeare's last direct descendant, his granddaughter, died in 1670.

The Real Macbeth

(c. 1005 - 1057 AD)

Macbeth is one of Shakespeare's most famous characters. Yet many people don't know that the story is based on events from history. It is thought that Shakespeare read early historical books which tell the history of England, Scotland and Ireland. However, he changed these historical events considerably, to make his play more entertaining for us, his audience.

Although it is impossible to know all the facts, according to history Mac Bethad (Macbeth) was King of Scotland from 1040 to 1057. The name 'Mac Bethad' means 'son of life'. It is actually an Irish name, not a Scottish name.

Scotland in the eleventh century was a cruel land to live in. It had many wars and mass killings occurred often. Whoever ruled Scotland had to protect family, community and the land from any enemies. However, many of a ruler's enemies were actually the people closest to him. These enemies were usually unhappy and jealous relatives, who wanted to be king themselves.

Enemies of the king would form a group and challenge the ruler. This happened because a king could choose the next king. In other words, kings didn't simply pass the rule straight onto their eldest son, or closest relative. In Mac Bethad's time, the king could choose who he wanted to replace them. Many

people were murdered by their jealous relatives.

Mac Bethad was born around 1005. He was the son of Findlaech mac Ruaidri, who was a High Steward in the north of Scotland. It is thought that Mac Bethad's mother was Donada, the second child of King Malcolm II. This means that Mac Bethad was the grandson of a king.

In 1020, Mac Bethad's father died. It is thought that he was murdered by his brother's son. Mac Bethad's cousin became High Steward. Twelve years later, Mac Bethad's cousin was killed as punishment for murdering Mac Bethad's father and Mac Bethad became High Steward.

Mac Bethad then married his cousin's widow, Gruoch (Lady Macbeth). She had one son, called Lulach. Gruoch was the granddaughter of Kenneth III. Their marriage meant that Mac Bethad had a very good claim to the Scottish throne.

However, Donnchad mac Crinain (King Duncan I) was the king already. Although Donnchad mac Crinain should have made friends with his unhappy relatives, including Mac Bethad, he didn't. This was a mistake. It meant that Mac Bethad finally killed Donnchad mac Crinain in 1040. One historical tale says that Mac Bethad and Banquo cleverly sent the king a sleeping potion and killed him

while he was asleep. Mac Bethad became king.

History states that Mac Bethad was a very good king. His kingdom became more stable and wealthier. Mac Bethad even travelled overseas while he was king, which shows how much confidence he had during his rule.

In 1054, Donnchad's son, Mael Coluim mac Donnchad (Malcolm), opposed Mac Bethad's rule. Mael Coluim and his supporters took control of southern Scotland. Three years later, in 1057, Mac Bethad's army finally lost against Mael Coluim's army. Mac Bethad was killed in battle. It is thought that he was buried in the graveyard at Saint Oran's Chapel on the Isle of Iona. He is the last of many kings to be buried there.

No one knows what happened to Mac Bethad's wife, Gruoch. In Shakespeare's play, she becomes insane and dies, although there is no historical account of what actually happened to her.

Unlike in Shakespeare's play, Mac Bethad's death didn't mean Duncan's son became king. First, the son of Gruoch, Lulach, became the Scottish ruler. However, Lulach was a weak king. His people laughed at him for being foolish. He was quickly murdered — and that's when Mael Coluim became king.

The Real Macbeth Family Tree

Key:
Parent of ——————
Married ══════

'Malcolm I'
King 943-954
Máel Coluim mac Domnaill

'Duff'
King 962-966
Duib mac Máel Coluim

'Kenneth II'
King 971-995
Cináeda mac Máel Coluim

Domnall

'Kenneth III'
King 997-1005
Cináeda mac Duib

'Malcolm II'
King 1005-1034
Máel Coluim mac Cináeda

Ruadri

First wife
- name
unknown — 1 — Boite mac Cináeda — 2 — Gruoch

Máel
Brigté

Mormaer of Moray
Findláech mac Ruaidrí

Donada

Bethoc
(eldest)

Máel
Coluim

Gille
Coemgáin — 1 — 'Lady Macbeth'
Gruoch ingen Boite — 2 — 'Macbeth'
King 1040-1057
Mac Bethad

'Duncan I'
King 1034-1040
Donnchad mac Crináin

Suthen

Lulach
King 1057-1058
'The Fool'

'Malcolm III'
King 1058-1093
Máel Coluim mac Donnchada

'Donald III'
King 1093-1097
Domnall Bán

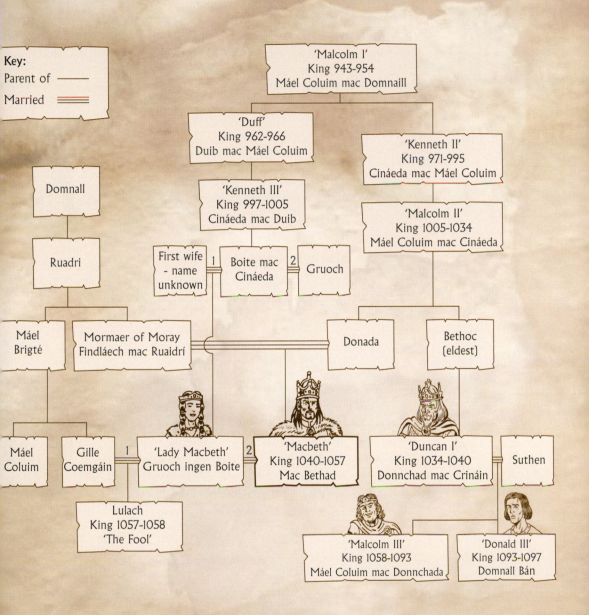

Major Characters

Macbeth, Thane of Glamis

Macbeth is a leader in the king's army, but he is not satisfied with this and greed makes him want even more success. He becomes the Thane of Cawdor aft defeating the Norwegians. The witches' predictions and his wife's encourageme lead him to kill Duncan and become King of Scotland. Although brave in batt he is an insecure and unfair ruler.

Lady Macbeth, Macbeth's wife

She wants power and wealth more than anything else and she encourages Macbeth to murder Duncan. In the end, her guilt makes her crazy and she suffers nightmares, starts sleepwalking and becomes obsessed with the blood on her hands which no one else can see.

Duncan, King of Scotland

He is a kind and trusting older king. His kindness allows Macbeth to attack hi Macbeth kills him (and his two guards) with a dagger. Duncan's death and his so escape means Macbeth is made king.

Malcolm and Donalbain, Duncan's sons

These two men are King Duncan's sons. When their father dies, they flee to avoid being murdered themselves. Donalbain escapes to Ireland. Malcolm goes to England, where he hopes to build an army to take back the kingdom from the evil Macbeth. At the end of the play, after Macbeth is defeated, Malcolm becomes king.

Three Witches, the Weird Sisters

The three witches have a very important role in this play. They tell Macbeth that he will be Thane of Cawdor, Tha of Glamis and eventually King. Their predictions lead Macbeth to commit many murders. At the same time, howev they predict that while Banquo may not be king, he will be happier and his sons will be kings. Later, they pred Macbeth's doom. Macbeth gets very confused by their predictions.

Major Characters

anquo, Leader in the King's army

e is a leader in Duncan's army along with Macbeth. He's also the subject of one of e witches' predictions. Unlike Macbeth, he does not act to fulfill these predictions. stead, he relies on his better judgment and morals. After Macbeth arranges his urder, Banquo reappears as a ghost, which represents the guilt and anguish Macbeth feeling over the murder.

Fleance

He is Banquo's son and the first in a line of kings as predicted by the Three Witches. He escapes when his father is killed. He represents a future Macbeth cannot bear: a line of kings following Banquo and not his own sons.

acduff, Thane of Fife

e is a Scottish nobleman who begins to question Macbeth's unfair rule. Macbeth ders that Macduff's wife and children are murdered. Macduff eventually joins Malcolm d the English forces to fight Macbeth and get revenge for the murders of his family. e witches tell Macbeth that he does not need to fear anyone 'born of a woman' owever Macduff was cut out of his mother's womb meaning that he wasn't actually rn of a woman. He is the man who kills Macbeth.

Siward, Earl of Northumberland

He is the leader of the English army and Duncan's brother. He leads an English army of ten thousand men against Macbeth. They disguise themselves with branches from Birnam Wood. He loses his son, Young Siward, to Macbeth.

ecate, The 'Queen' Witch

e demands loyalty and respect of the Three Witches. She makes fun of the Three Witches for helping an ungrateful acbeth. She later commands them to tell Macbeth his future according to her will.

Link Map of Characters in Shakespeare's Macbeth

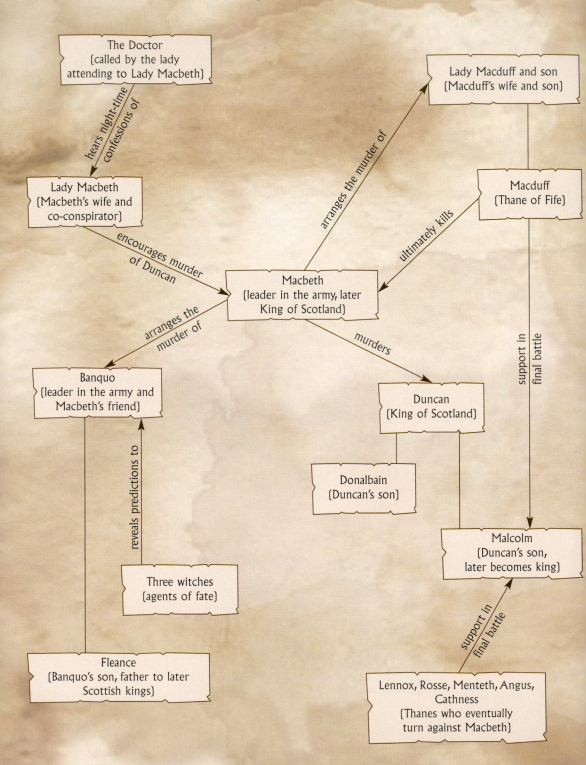

The Doctor
(called by the lady
attending to Lady Macbeth)

hears night-time confessions of

Lady Macbeth
(Macbeth's wife and
co-conspirator)

encourages murder
of Duncan

Lady Macduff and son
(Macduff's wife and son)

Macduff
(Thane of Fife)

arranges the murder of

ultimately kills

Macbeth
(leader in the army, later
King of Scotland)

arranges the
murder of

murders

support in
final battle

Banquo
(leader in the army and
Macbeth's friend)

reveals predictions to

Duncan
(King of Scotland)

Donalbain
(Duncan's son)

Three witches
(agents of fate)

Malcolm
(Duncan's son,
later becomes king)

support in
final battle

Fleance
(Banquo's son, father to later
Scottish kings)

Lennox, Rosse, Menteth, Angus,
Cathness
(Thanes who eventually
turn against Macbeth)

Famous Quotations from Shakespeare's Macbeth

Location in play	Shakespeare's Original	ELT Version	Meaning
Act 1 Scene 1 Page 8	'When shall we three meet again? In thunder, lightning, or in rain? When the hurly-burly's done, When the battle's lost and won.'	'When shall we three meet again? In heavy storm or pouring rain? When one side's lost and the other's won.'	The three witches say this at the start of the play. They are predicting when they will meet with Macbeth and Banquo, and tell each man of his future. Their meeting will begin the trouble that leads to the multiple murders of this play.
Act 1 Scene 1 Page 8	'Fair is foul, and foul is fair.'	'Fair is dark and dark is fair.'	The three witches say this at the beginning of the play. They are telling of the coming events where good and evil will be turned upside down; when fair play will be destructive, and destruction will create fairness. Not long afterwards, Macbeth says in Act One, Scene Three that he has never seen such a foul and fair day before (both a good and bad day).
Act 1 Scene 3 Page 18	'If chance will have me King, why chance may crown me, Without my stir.'	'If I'm going to be king, it'll happen by itself.'	Macbeth thinks this out loud after hearing the three witches predict that he will be made king. He is thinking that he doesn't need to do anything but wait, and it will happen. In the end, however, this is what Banquo chooses to do, while Macbeth chooses to take it into his own hands and make it happen by murdering King Duncan.
Act 1 Scene 5 Page 20	'Yet do I fear thy nature: It is too full o'the milk of human-kindness.'	'But you're too kind to do what you have to do to become king.'	Lady Macbeth says this as she reads a letter from her husband. In it, he is telling his wife about how the three witches predicted that he will be king. However, Lady Macbeth believes her husband is too weak, too kind and too gentle to do what he must do to become king: murder Duncan.
Act 1 Scene 5 Page 22	'Look like the innocent flower, But be the serpent under't.'	'You mustn't let people know what you're planning. You must welcome him properly.'	Lady Macbeth tells her husband to look sweet like a flower but to really be the snake (serpent) that is underneath the flower. She tells him that he should be very careful and to make sure nobody realises that he is planning to become king by murder and lies.
Act 2 Scene 1 Page 31	'Is this a dagger which I see before me, The handle toward my hand?'	'Is this a dagger I can see? Come here! Let me hold you!'	Macbeth thinks he sees a dagger in front of him. He feels it is telling him to use it to stab his king. However, he fears this dagger is not real, but just something he imagines is there. It is as he is thinking all this that he uses a dagger to kill King Duncan.
Act 2 Scene 2 Page 36	'Will all great Neptune's ocean wash this blood Clean from my hand? No - this my hand will rather the multitudinous seas incarnadine, Making the green one red.'	'All the water in the ocean won't wash away this blood from my hands.'	Macbeth says this to his wife after he has killed King Duncan. He feels terribly guilty, and worries that the guilt will never disappear. His words are echoed later in Lady Macbeth's cries that she has blood on her hands.

Famous Quotations from Shakespeare's Macbeth

Location in play	Shakespeare's Original	ELT Version	Meaning
Act 2 Scene 3 Page 45	'There's daggers in men's smiles.'	'Here there are knives in men's smiles.'	Donalbain says this after realising that his father, King Duncan, and his father's guards, have been murdered. He and his brother Malcolm are suspicious of who killed their father, and do not trust anyone, least of all the people who claim to be helping them get revenge for their father's death.
Act 4 Scene 1 Page 78	'Double, double toil and trouble; Fire burn, and cauldron bubble.'	'Double, double toil and trouble, Fire, burn, and make all bubble.'	The three witches chant this spell as they dance around the potion they are cooking on the fire. They want to double the amount of trouble about to happen. Their words increase the audience's anticipation that the action is about reach a high point.
Act 5 Scene 1 Page 105	'Out, damned spot! Out, I say!'	'Out! Out, I say!'	Lady Macbeth cries this as she tries desperately to clean her hands. She is sleepwalking, and believes her hands are covered in blood. Her guilt causes her to see this blood, for the doctor and servant watching tell the reader that her hands are clean already.
Act 5 Scene 1 Page 106	' … all the perfumes of Arabia will not sweeten this little hand.'	'I can still smell the blood. Nothing will make my little hand smell sweet again.'	Lady Macbeth continues to talk as she sleepwalks in this scene. She repeats again and again that her hands are stained with blood, and truly believes, in her sleep, that she will never be able to wash her hands of their dirty, guilty secret.
Act 5 Scene 5 Page 118	'Out, out, brief candle! Life's but a walking shadow, a poor player That struts and frets his hour upon the stage, And then is heard no more. It is a tale told by an idiot, full of sound and fury, signifying nothing.'	'Life is but a walking shadow. It's a story that a fool tells — full of noise but with no meaning.'	Macbeth cries this out in sadness and despair when he learns that his wife, the Queen, is dead. He has realised that life is short, and often finished before it even begins. It is a bleak and remorseful view, for he now thinks that while life appears to contain much promise, it is actually empty and meaningless.

Notes

Notes

Notes

CD Track Listings

Macbeth

Track 1	Copyright Notice
Track 2	Introduction
Track 3	Act 1 Scene 1
Track 4	Act 1 Scene 2
Track 5	Act 1 Scene 3
Track 6	Act 1 Scene 4
Track 7	Act 1 Scene 5
Track 8	Act 1 Scene 6
Track 9	Act 1 Scene 7
Track 10	Act 2 Scene 1
Track 11	Act 2 Scene 2
Track 12	Act 2 Scene 3
Track 13	Act 2 Scene 4
Track 14	Act 3 Scene 1
Track 15	Act 3 Scene 2
Track 16	Act 3 Scene 3
Track 17	Act 3 Scene 4
Track 18	Act 3 Scene 5
Track 19	Act 3 Scene 6
Track 20	Act 4 Scene 1
Track 21	Act 4 Scene 2
Track 22	Act 4 Scene 3
Track 23	Act 5 Scene 1
Track 24	Act 5 Scene 2
Track 25	Act 5 Scene 3
Track 26	Act 5 Scene 4
Track 27	Act 5 Scene 5
Track 28	Act 5 Scene 6
Track 29	Act 5 Scene 7
Track 30	Act 5 Scene 8

OTHER CLASSICAL COMICS TITLES:

Henry V	Frankenstein	Great Expectations	Jane Eyre
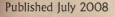			
Published July 2008	Published Autumn 2008	Published Autumn 2008	Published Early 2009